Chronicles of a Mother to Her Son

EDINA S. KUJA

Chronicles of a Mother to Her Son

Copyright © 2021 by Edina S. Kuja

Paperback ISBN: 978-1-952098-77-2

Printed in the United States of America. All rights reserved solely by the publisher. This book or parts thereof may not be reproduced in any form, stored in a retrieval system, or transmitted in any form by any means - electronic, mechanical, photocopy. Unless otherwise noted, Bible quotations are taken from the Holy Bible, King James Version. Copyright 1982 by Thomas Nelson, Inc., publishers. Used by permission.

Published by:
Cornerstone Publishing
A Division of Cornerstone Creativity Group LLC
Info@thecornerstonepublishers.com
www.thecornerstonepublishers.com
516.547.4999

Author's Contact

For booking to speak at your next event or to order bulk copies of this book please send email to:

ednasichalwe@gmail.com

CONTENTS

Dedication..5

Acknowledgments......................................7

Preface..9

A Gift to You..11

1. My perception of you........................13
2. My experience with you.....................15
3. You are important.............................19
4. Where you come from.......................23
5. Challenges..25
6. Manhood.. 29
7. Character..33
8. Love your wife..................................37
9. Raising children.................................41
10. People..45
11. Church...51
12. Purpose-driven Life...........................53
13. Leadership....................................... 56

14. Finances..57
15. Health..59

See you later note...62
My prayer..63
References..64

About the Author..65

DEDICATION

I dedicate this book to you because it is too amazing to miss reading it.

ACKNOWLEDGMENTS

I am very much thankful to everyone who supported and was committed to this project to its accomplishment. I am eternally grateful to my Heavenly Father for giving me the breath of life, strength to write, health to be able to sit down and work on this book. Also, for giving me these amazing rewards of three brilliant boys, the bible says, 'children are rewards from God.' Indeed, I am grateful and delightful, they are the reason I wrote this book.

I am also appreciative for you who bought this book online or a hard copy and have this book in your hands right now. I will be ungrateful if I don't thank my husband for his never-ending love and support, not to mention the opportunity of making me the mother of his children. Finally, many thanks to my boys Divine, Diline, and Wilson Kuja Jr. for allowing me to be their mother.

PREFACE

This is a book that has no boundaries to be read by anyone and everyone. It is a mixture of narrative and poetic styles but delivers an intimate message from a mother to her son. It can be read by every religion, dominion, and gender. The book explains the feelings, teachings, instructions, and expectations of a mother to her son. It tells the wisdom of a mother as she experiences and evaluates raising children from infanthood and as she imagines their adulthood.

The book aims to comfort and to communicate to every son who has never experienced or doesn't know motherly love, thoughts, and prayers. It also portrays, gives advice and opinions on the things that children will pass through from a motherly perspective. The book has stories, warnings, advice, anecdotes, sermons, and lessons, and at the end of the book, a prayer. It shows perspectives and practices of parenthood.

It also connects the conversations that a parent and a child make as they grow together. And lastly, the amazing thing about the book is, it reflects God's love in motherly love. It is the book for everyone to learn and relearn about different perspectives of life despite the fact that the son is the main character.

A GIFT TO YOU

I might be or not alive when you are reading this book. But this book is one of the gifts I wanted to give you in case I die today. I thought it might be important than any material thing to give to you, my son. I tried to study as much as I could to make sure I had something worthy for you to inherit, but If I die trying, please just receive this book as an expensive token from me. It is my wish always to be with you, and talk to you, and have some discussions with you, trying to understand you, teach you about life, seeing you grow, making decisions, making mistakes, and learning from them, who will be your girlfriends and best friends, who will you marry, not to mention seeing my grandchildren and always praying for you.

I might not be there as you live your life, but perhaps this book will be there, and you might go back to it and see what I think about anything that I will be able to put in here. As I am living my life, I always think about what new thing I learned today that I will need to pass to my children and to future generations.

It might be old by the time you guys grow up because the world is changing every single day, and it is changing fast. But maybe you can use my two cents to learn something that can be applied in your life.

1
MY PERCEPTION OF YOU

Since you were born, you have brightened my life in an unexplainable special way. You changed my life completely, shaped my characters and overtook my thoughts. You made me realize there is another self-outside my body. A person that I think about first before me, putting him first before my everything. I thank God that I had a chance to see you, hold you, and raise you. I see the manifestation of the goodness and faithfulness of God as He gave me this precious reward.

Since you were in my womb, I wanted to tell you more with my lips closed. Your dad knows I talk a lot when I write than when I open my lips. I thought a lot about you and how you will be a giant human being in this World. And I believe this is what God is telling me in advance about your impact in this world. When I think maybe that's it, more and more revelations and more information is coming to my mind as I see you grow. They are still coming, and I want to put them in writing so that when I return to my Heavenly Father, you will have my thoughts with you at your hands, device, or whatever gadget you will be using. So that you don't forget how I thought you would become. Sons, this is not my debt to you, and please don't feel you are obligated to any of my writings. I can say this is only my fantasy about you, but it is what I pray for every day. Can a mother dream of her boys? Yes I have that right to do so. Love, this word in writing is not enough to express how I feel about you. But as it is the only vocabulary available so far, I should probably use it. Perhaps you will come up with another vocabulary that explains how I feel about you when you have children of your own. I might not say it enough when you were growing up, but you are loved. I remember the song I used to sing to you when you were infant.

'Didi Divine, your father, loves you;

your mother loves you too.

They both love you so, so, so much *2'

2
MY EXPERIENCE WITH YOU

Son, I just want to share the good experience I have had with you. This is the motherly experience, care, and love to her son. To you, it might be the same experience, the same care and love to your children but manifested in different ways. I will ask my mother one day, is this the way she felt when she had me?

> I loved how I fell for you since you were in my womb. I just love this love. It is so pure and so tender but so deep and so genuine. Since I had you, I learned the actual meaning of love, understanding, and patience. I love the way I love taking care of you the best way I can.

> I love the way I am not happy when you misbehave or do something wrong.

> I love the way I always want to protect you with all I am and all I have.

> I love the way I feel sad and responsible whenever I fail to meet your needs or your expectations.

> I love the way I feel guilt and want to punish myself whenever I don't do my responsibility like a mother.

> I love the way I wake up in the morning and

prepare you to go to school. Sometimes I would want to sleep a little because I just came from night shift work but just doing it rejuvenated my energy.

I love the way I feel when you were little, hugging me and putting your hands around my neck. Oooh, did I mention that is the best feeling ever? I would want to get it all the time. I wish I would put it in your daily chores, or as a grown-up, one of your to-do lists. But then it just felt so natural and beautiful when you did it without requests. I wonder if this is the reason why God wanted humanity to decide to love him and not force them to.

I smile when I remember carrying you around and playing with you.

I love when I grin at you, and your charming eyes rekindle my sobbing heart when i am sad or hurt.

I love the way I celebrate when I see your success and accomplish your milestones. I sometimes wonder is it possible for someone else to love you the way I do. Or is it possible for me to love another person the way I do to you?

I love the way I invigorate and strengthen whenever I see your smile. I love the feeling of you calling me the magic word 'mama' because it reminds me of my responsibility and the irreplaceable position in your life. Sometimes i ask myself, is this how God loves us? The bible says a mother forget the baby at her breast and have no compassion on the child she has borne? Though she may forget, I will not forget you![1]. God must love us so deeply since it is an addition to that of motherly love.

I love the way I want to know you and learn how to raise you right.

I love the way I am concerned about whatever you do so that I can try to save me and you from future regrets.

I love the way I can go the extra mile and beyond my capabilities to make sure you are ok.

I love the way you make me read the bible and pray just to make sure your life is secured in God's hands. I believe and pray to God to make me a decent mother and to make you an excellent and successful son.

I love the way you taught me to love others because of the love I have for you. I love the way you make me patient with others because I will always be patient with you.

I love the way you indirectly discipline and shape my characters because I want to be a good role model for you.

I love the way you made me study because I wanted to set up a higher standards for you.

I love the way you motivate my wake up in the morning and go to work because we both need food on the table.

I love the way you make me understand people because of the way I need to understand you.

I love the way you make me selfless.

I love the way I have these optimistic ideas about your future, and here is where I understand how a lot of things have a role to play in your future.

I love the way I feel when I watch you sleep peacefully.

I love the way It hurts me when I punish you.

I love the way you make me creative just to figure out what different meals I can cook for you and make sure it is delicious and healthy too.

I love the way you make me desperate just to make sure you turn out to be a brilliant decent boy.

I just love the way you make me see the world in different pairs of lenses with your love.

Son, whenever you see I fall short, I have done my best. And whenever you see I missed, perhaps I was busy working on other areas more and failed to focus on that particular area.

3
YOU ARE IMPORTANT

Son, you are born to be great, the definition of greatness. You are far away from being a normal human being. You were created from God's image. You are only you to this World. No one will be like you or will ever be like you. You are unique and God's masterpiece. Create your followers that when you are body is buried in the soil, your spirit still lives in this World. Others will want to be like you, learn from you, and appreciate your remarkable legacy. I saw you as giant even when you had that tiny body of an infant boy.

Don't let anyone make you to feel devalued, you don't matter, or you are not important. This might be their perspective of you, which doesn't change the truth that you do matter, and you are important. They might not recognize you, and actually, they might even fight you. Sometimes you might think people hate you, but on the contrary, they are just scared of you. They are intimidated because they know you are unstoppable when you strive to be one.

They might not celebrate you or even appreciate you, but that should not stop you from being the best version of yourself that you can be. They might act like they don't see you, but that should not make you discouraged. Continue to embrace who you are and your becoming process.

> You don't have to preach to anyone that you are important.
>
> You don't have to show anybody that you are important.
>
> You don't have to threaten others to let them know that you are important.
>
> You don't have to always search for attention to let people know that you are important.
>
> You don't have to whine, cry to show people you are important.
>
> You don't have to prove yourself that you are important.
>
> You must be important for God himself to come to this dusty world for you. You must be important for Someone to sacrifice his heaven life for you. You must be important for Someone to pass through the disgraceful death for you. You must be important for God to have a meeting in heaven on how to save you. You must be important for Jesus to hang on in this world for 33 years just to fulfill his purpose of redeeming you. You must be important for

Someone to send his beloved son to die just for your salvation.

It must be important for someone to think about you and your future. You don't have to demonstrate anything to show anybody you are important, or you don't have to sell your soul just to be approved, fit in, or admired. You are too important and great to fit in anybody's box. You were created to stand out, which is why no one has your fingerprints.

Son, you don't have to be someone else to be important. You have been created uniquely, the bible says, *'But you are a chosen race, a royal priesthood, a holy nation, a people for his possession, that you may proclaim the excellencies of him who called you out of darkness into his marvelous light.[2]* You don't have to be her/him. You don't need to like what others like. You don't need to hate what others hate. You don't have to be in the same generation or have the same color as someone or to have the same thought with others. You don't have to be in a certain religion or be in one religion with someone or having the same perspective with someone.

You fit yourself. You don't have to fit someone else. You are the best when you be yourself, than being someone else. Love yourself and always want to be the best version of yourself. This doesn't mean you should not have mentors or learn from others, just make sure what you learn from others refine and unleash your potentials and bring the best version of you. If you would have to, just remind them you are present by being the solution that they are looking for. You are important by being the best at what you do than them.

4
WHERE YOU COME FROM

I know the world will tell you where you came from, how is your country and what kind of people are living there. Sons, articulate this beyond the borders, beyond the walls and lines that people put on the land. But I will not stop you from thinking of where you originally come from. This is what I will tell you about where you truly come from....

> Where you came from, children respect their elders.
>
> Where you came from, we face our problems heads on and not running away from them.
>
> Where you came from, we take responsibility and be accountable for our mistakes.
>
> Where you came from, we don't make excuses on deciding our journey, time frame, or destination
>
> Where you came from, we don't try to find someone to blame for our misfortunes. We face them and find the solution to them.
>
> Where you came from, we fell once, twice, more than three times, and we wake up again, clean our specks of dust and keep moving.

Where you came from, we prepare, not only for the planned and unplanned too, but we also don't hate surprises. On the contrary, we do love them. They sharpen our brains.

Where you came from, men provide and protect their families.

Where you came from, we love each other beyond our colors, races, religion, or tribes.

Where you came from, we don't envy each other. We challenge one another.

Where you came from, we rule the world with intelligence and character and not spill blood, power, force or manipulations.

Where you came from, we subdue life with resilience and hardworking.

Where you came from, we see success with results, wisdom and patience.

Where you came from, we don't only base it on the history and resentments, we rewrite the history, and without grudges, we bury the negative statistics.

Son honor the sacrifice of your ancestors, include your parents with excellence.

5
CHALLENGES

Son, a smooth sea never made a skilled sailor. Son, you are born to be a problem solver. Every time you see a challenge, or a test, it is the opportunity to manifest what God has created in you in the first place. You are God's ambassador, with him, you can do all things. Always think of problems and challenges as a prospect to unleash and unmask your potential, an opportunity to be Great, a time to brainstorm until you get the solution. Remember, when you reach the end of contemplation, that is where God starts. Everyone in this world has been given an assignment to do. And as Dr. Myles Munroe says, life without a purpose is time wastage. I believe when God created you and had me kept you 9 months in my womb, He had an assignment for you to do in this World. Other's call it destiny, and the best measurement of destiny is time. Don't rest until you know what is your assignment and accomplish it. And life is the only timeframe you have to do that.

Never walk away from the problem unless otherwise walking away is the solution of the problem. Face the problem, solve it. This will help you to have the experience to solve other problems. But it will also give you the confidence to tackle future problems. When you walk away from the problem, you are also creating a walk-away experience to other problems. Problems are part of our being. Being a conqueror or failure is a combination of preparation, experience, determination, courage, and decision. Once Michael Jordan said, "I have failed over and over and over in my life, and that is why I succeeded." Create your disciples and generation of winners. But it just feels good that you lose while trying not to lose when you didn't even try to solve it. The loser of all is the one who failed to try.

Son, heal your wounds with hope and faith and don't let past pain be the point of your reference. Shine your crown with integrity and love. Walk your path in life with diligence. Leave the footsteps to your sons and grandsons to follow it. Invest your energy and strength in achieving greatness. Correct the negative trends and patterns with new methodologies of a changed and transformed life.

I am still thinking that the world is beautiful. The only challenge is its inhabitants. Not all people are good, and life is hard. There are no shortcuts. One thing that is guaranteed is adversity and tribulation. Just remember, God doesn't put us through anything that we cannot handle.

Son, accept backlash and criticism because there is nothing you can do in this world to be perfect and approved by everyone. Even Jesus himself was killed despite doing all good and being loved by God and humankind. Challenging enough is, in the current digital and social media world, the platform of bullying is so wide. Be aware of this because not all the time you will be able to justify yourself. Sometimes you won't, and you still need to ignore and keep going. One day Hillary Clinton said, "learn how to take criticism seriously but not personally."

There are no such people as superheroes. Don't be hard on yourself when you fall short. This only means to remain humble and remind yourself that you are still a human. The beauty of falling short is it gives you time to refuel, restore, rejuvenate your life as you examine your failures. It can also give you a chance to start over. The process is called experience, which cultivates the roots of stewardship and wisdom.

6
MANHOOD

TD Jakes, in his book He-motions, said, self-discovery is a vital part of human development (pg. 37). I am the last person to tell you about manhood as I am a woman. I can only tell you about him as a mother. Son, there are a lot of definitions of a man, especially when it comes to gender roles. The most definition used is of social responsibilities. It has been changing throughout the generations and generations. Before World War 2, a male version of a human being was the one who goes to work, and provides for his family. And with that situation in those what we call ancient days, a woman's role was in the house, taking care of the children, and managing a household. It is not this way anymore, and perhaps it will change by the time you have your family. Son, men are not breadwinners anymore. Women can be breadwinners too. But this should not stop you to be a breadwinner, you just need to be the great one to lead. Men take care of their kids, too, the same way women do. This should not make you feel you betray your gender or inferior at all. This is the time to make an impact to your children. Plant your wisdom in them every chance you get. Son, now men also belong in the kitchen. Remember the time he stepped in and gave you guys a shower when I was occupied. Or when he cleaned the table and washed the dishes. As the Jaluo guy raised in Manilla, where people are very conservative and specific about the man and woman role in the households; dishes and taking care of the children are the women's responsibilities even to this day. This doesn't take off your manhood. On the contrary, it makes you the best husband, and father, your wife and children look up to.

Currently, some men are confused, as what they used to do to showcase their manhood is being done with the women. Many define who they are by what they do. But I am telling you that not always what you do defines who you are. There is a big reason why you are physically different from a woman. And perhaps in the community, the physical difference might not be significant. But this is what I think, The last thing the world doesn't consider might be the first thing God does consider. So, before you start dancing to the tune of the gender roles which is being defined by the community surrounding us, or social orientation, consider that. Descriptions according to the community changes, because there are a gazillion communities everywhere you go in the world. Establish your definition of a man that will not change when you are in Africa or Scandinavia, whether in Jamaica or the United States of America. If you feel confused, go back to the basics and ask for wisdom from your highest Man above, the one who created a man. Nobody should give you a definition of yourself than yourself. Know yourself and treat yourself accordingly. Treat and behave yourself as King, and others will treat you the same. Let the situations and environment reveal what kind of a King you are. Prove yourself the best man in front of other men, not in front of women; it is too obvious. Don't hurt or abuse women. They are all you got to push you, motivate you, and cheer you up. Always be the best man out of the rest. Become what you respect and be a good man, but don't waste time proving it.

I don't have the right and accurate answer, and, in my generation, we might have a certain definition and expectations of who a man is. But perhaps it will already be expired in Your century or after 20 to 30 years to come. Only one thing does not change the Word of God. Son, get your definition of a Man there. Never stand idly because silence of good people is as bad as the voices of bad people. I hope I raised you a warrior, and a defender, a man of courage and not a coward. Don't be a man of plans and intentions, but a man who puts those plans and intentions into actions.

So whatever field you will choose, whether in a screen, factors, behind the computer, on a construction job, beside patients, in front of the students, playing with machines, or in a farm, don't complain, whine, don't gossip or be mad about some dude being paid more. Be the man that will do your absolute best to paint your masterwork no matter what job you do. Be the same man of integrity, honor, and character, whether you are a janitor or CEO making millions and employing thousands. Put your head down and hustle. Don't look for praise, or approval, or don't wish you were in someone else's shoes. Be grateful that you are alive, and use each day to keep the fire burning. And always remember above the soil or under the soil, I cheer you up, clap for you, and I am always proud of you.

7
CHARACTER

Son, character is the very important thing in your life. People are watching what you do more than what you say. In everything you do, know that character is part and parcel of your journey. Character can bring down everything you have built all your life. Character can erase every memory and every history you have made. Character can make you sit with giants, and character can promote you. There are very popular people who did mega things in this world, but today we don't remember them because of those things, but we remember them because of their character downfall. Men with characters in this world have become endangered species. I want to give an example of US President Clinton. The only thing that the world is remembering about when you mention his name is his scandal with Monica Renwick. It is the story that passing-through generations and generations. Character is simply showing who you are when you are alone, portraying when you are with other people. And currently, son, you can't really guarantee privacy. Camera and digital widgets are plenty everywhere. It is so easy for what you think you do alone to be exposed on the public without your notice, by the time you see it, the world has already seen it, and you are the last one to get it. Sometimes people confuse character and image. Image is what you portray in public, but character is who you are when you are alone. Do you remember the story of Samson in the bible? The popular part of it is how he was manipulated by Delilah, and mostly forgotten, the part that he was the powerful individual on this earth. And the bad thing about character, sometimes it only needs one wrong act to mess up the rest of your good acts. Live wisely son.

Son, you don't have to be famous like Jesus or layman barber in Manila, Mara Tanzania. You don't have to be a president like Trump or have daily scandals. You don't have to win a noble prize like Mother Theresa or be a terrorist legend like Osama Bin Laden. You don't have to be a wealthier man in the world like Bill Gates or a small-scale farmer in Msangano Village, Mbeya Tanzania. You don't have to be successful like Beyonce or a preacher like TD Jakes. It might not be on the screens, newspapers, social media or magazines, but people are watching you.

> It can be to admire you or to expose you.
>
> It can be for their own self benefits or for your own safe benefits.

It can be for a wrong reason or for the right one.

It might be to help you, protect you or to report you.

It can be whether you fail or win or defeating challenges.

You make them decide what page of your life they will write.

It might be a second, or for some weeks. It might be for a year, a moment, for a short time or for a lifetime, but everyone around you has something to say about you because they are watching you.

Some are watching you to be inspired, others to destroy you.

Some are watching you to encourage you, others to criticize you and find something wrong with you.

Some are watching you to laugh at you, others to wait for you, and see your results.

Some are watching you to learn from you, others to copy you, and unlearn from you.

Some to compare you, others to shut you down.

Some to love you, and others to hate you, but they will still be watching you.

Whether you have a choice or live with no purpose, create your own unique story because someone is watching you.

It might be the son, may be a neighbor, definitely a father, obviously a mother, sometimes siblings, other times colleagues, rarely acquaintances, often your roommates; most of the time your friends, and even the public. I just want to let you know she is watching. He is watching. Someone is watching.

8
LOVE YOUR WIFE

I might not be the ideal individual to talk to you about choosing a good wife. Please have some time to read Proverbs 31. It gives you guidance on who you might be looking for. That is the proverb of a mother who told her son about getting the right woman. It might be a good cheat sheet when you get to experience that journey. But before that, make sure you focus on being a good husband.

Son, sometimes love is the most complicated word and thing to talk about for me. This will be a good topic your dad would want to talk to you about. Perhaps you already have these conversations or have them in the future. All I can share is all I experience as a wife. But all I know is, there is no love in selfishness. And don't allow selfishness to pull you away from your wife's and children's love. Do you remember when your dad took you to the malls to find my gifts? Gifts light up the souls and brighten the eyes and heart. Sometimes it is not how much they cost, it's the feeling they bring that someone thought about you, that value the most. The beauty and value of the gift are not when you have plenty and just give extra, but when you have nothing and still give something.

Remember every day when we pray together in the evenings before we go to sleep. I loved it when your father pray, I listen to every word he altered to God, like an employee reporting to his employer, representing his family to the higher authority, that he is accounted for. Be the priest of your household son.

I know you might not see this more often now as I have a different working schedule, but your father used to cook for me on Sundays. It was not the taste of the food that interested me but the deliciousness of the loving act, spiced with care when he was making the food that devoured me and made my heart flattered. Love your wife, serve her, defend her, listen to her, protect her, enable her, uplift her, fight for her, play with her, pray for and with her. And make sure your sons see this because this is something that cannot be taught by words, rather by actions.

I don't share these with you to brag about them. I just give you examples of the things that would make a wife thrilled and appreciate you. A wife needs to know that you do love her and, most important, you care for her. This is not only a matter of heart, but it is also the manifestations and acts. Son, quote me accurately. I said you don't have to do the same or not doing them. Just decide on the best way to improve and update them and remain as natural as you can be. This is not the template. You do your ways according to her definition of love, care, and happiness. Words cannot give a real meaning of being a man of the house, or the head of the family as the bible refers, or actual looks, or the tenderness or toughness hat it requires, but just be the yin to her yang, the masculine to her feminine and to your sons as well.

Son, make your wife special. Don't do anything special that you do to her to any other woman. Because that will be public service and not to a special person anymore. Don't allow anything or anyone to compromise her position in your heart, inside your house, and outside your house. Do not use the money to control or manipulate her or define your authority over her because that will be what you taught her to do to you when she has money herself—or cultivating the zeal to find money so she can relate to what you do to her. Your wife is your partner, not your competitor. You should be her best cheerleader and the number one to criticize her with love when you have different thoughts of things. Complement your wife not only inside your rooms but mostly outside. It soothes the heart and builds confidence in her. I can give you a reference written by your father, a Facebook post of June 2018 from your father.

> "To my love, my partner, the lady who makes the world respect me, Edna S. Kuja, thank you for brightening my day. I took time to read everybody's message as I think about God's Mercy. 5 months ago, I wouldn't have had a chance to do this. Thank you, Darling. I would love my boys to know a good woman from their mother. You are God-sent, and I can't thank you enough, darling. I can't wait for your birthday to get u back!
>
> Love you!"

Oooh, this text sounds grateful and tastes delicious. It is one of the texts I kept in my archives from your father. What will your wife keep in her archives?

9
RAISING CHILDREN

One thing I discovered is, raising children is a project of its own. Trying your best to do what you can do, hoping that you did the best and the impact will make sense. This reminded me of why Jesus said *I am sending you out like sheep among wolves. Therefore, be as shrewd as snakes and as innocent as doves.[3]* Today, I understand that when you raise children, you don't only raise them for you, but you raise them for the world. This is a big obligation because the test of how good you raise them is the reflection and manifestation of their characters in the community or when they play with others.

Perhaps when you grow up, you will see there are things I didn't do right, or I didn't raise you well. Know this, I tried to the best of my ability. I did the way I knew it was right with the help of the bible, some books, my own childhood experience, friends, relatives, and everything I knew. One day you will also have your children. Perhaps some of the things in these chronicles will make sense to you by then.

Relationship with your kids' matter, and is something

you will need your father's input on too, as you will just hear one side from me. Son, as I told you, you are a man. I cannot tell you how to relate to your kids as a man. All I can do is to share with you how I observed your father do it in addition to what I did. Whenever you feel disappointed by him, fall short, feel a gap or look at his weakness, just know it from me. I have witnessed him do the best he could, the best he knew how to give you the finest. Don't forget he had decisions and options, whether they are good or bad. The moments, to see the best version of your father, smiling, laughing, expressing his ego, is when he is with you.

He had an option not to fight whenever the setbacks came our way, but he never surrendered. He had an option not to work, but he did work very hard. Sometimes he couldn't get enough sleep. He was the one waking up very early in the morning and went straight to his home office or field office and always slept late. He had an option not to be patient with you, not to understand you, or not to stay with you, but He did and is still doing it. The fact that you had him around should make you the luckiest and favored child.

In Tanzania, some children are known as street children. Recently, they called them vulnerable children after stopped ignoring the fact that no street give birth to a child. These are children who survive by begging, sleeping, and living their lives in the streets. They also had or have fathers that have chosen the bad options. Some of them might not get lucky to ever see their fathers. Some are orphans, and some are not, just abandoned by their parents. And one thing that most people forget is, there can also be street/vulnerable children in big mansions, fancy homes, and expensive gates who fall in the category of abandoned children. This can also be the case for the orphan children when we stick to the definition of an orphan who lost their father and mother. But literally, there are a lot of orphans who are in the state of being, never lost a mother and father, they just left physically and deserted emotionally. Son, what I am trying to say is, you will always have options, just try your best to do the good ones. Life is full of decisions. Good or bad decisions from those options will make a good or bad life, not only for you, but for your family and generation as well.

One thing I will always be sure of is, since we got you, your father changed his life completely. Everything he was talking about, everything he was thinking about, and everything he could do, were for the future of his kids. He fought many wars, he stretched himself to the last point and gave himself many times for you, son. He is like having this picture of the best human being you will be and that he is responsible for giving you whatever you would need to get there. Son, you cannot protect your sons from dysfunctional behavior by expensive secured gates. You can only protect them from thieves who will come to steal properties and perhaps kill or injure them. To protect them from external fears is good but never forget to protect their internal esteem. And he who can be a good son will absolutely make a good father.

10
PEOPLE

Son, don't hate people; you are allowed to hate their bad behaviors or characters but respect all people. Before you judge anybody as per your perspective, give them a benefit of the doubt to understand them. There is nothing you can do without people. The best wealth of all is having people. I know today's world is teaching and preaching selfishness but trust me, those selfish also use people. Son, you need people in every area of your life. Anything that you will do, you will have to relate to people, whether it is business, whether it is an office, whether it is education or any field in life. If you don't meet them in everyday life, you will communicate with them. If not inside your house, then outside your house. One thing that you must remember is to try your best to value them, respect, care and love them. If God loves them to the point of sending one of His trinity parts, His beloved son, to just dying for them because they mess up. It was not because they are holy, good, and pure. On the contrary, they are walking opposite with the purpose of their creation. This should make you understand that they are very valuable to God. Once David asked God, *what is a man that you are mindful of him, the son of man that you care for him?*[4]

Expect nothing when you help anyone, include your family. Success is determined by how many lives you have touched. Being famous is a good smile of the heart, but only when it comes from the lips of people who mention your name to God as to thank Him for your existence. Maintain that popularity because it has no season, as it is within you, it is from who you are. Son, when you live your life with people, you have an account with them. Having time to interact with people means an opportunity to deposit or withdraw from that account. Deposit good deeds to people, so when you do wrong, you don't get an overdraft. Because at one time in life, you will. And remember, sometimes overdrafts have charges. Don't get used to it, and always withdraw is not as good as deposit. So, make sure you have enough deposits in your account.

Son, you cannot despise anybody. Never look down on anybody because you don't know who will help you in times of trouble. It doesn't matter the status, religion, color, or political identity. And be very careful with hate, because when you are done hating everyone, you will hate yourself. By the way, when you are stereotyping everything, you will never identify and appreciate uniqueness. The beauty of learning about people, be open-minded and let your brain reason and your responses filter. Son, family doesn't have to be limited with the biological relations, or where you came from, as the only definition of the family. In life, sometimes, the one you call real family might be very far away from you geographically, physically, and emotionally. But you can get people whom you treat each other like one. Family with no background, never looks alike, has different shapes, different cultures and characters. A family where you don't share sir names, don't even come from the same region, country, or continent, and different perspectives and opinions, but still there is genuine respect, love, and care. That is how you appreciate the beauty of diversity. The value of a good relationship is priceless, and when it comes to you, embrace it, nurture it, savor it and try to maintain it by all possible means.

Son, when you get a chance to be in a higher position, use the opportunity with humility. Respect the position you are in; respect people who trusted you for the position, respect those who taught you and those who were your predecessors. We are living in a different world, the world we created with our own hands. I sometimes think maybe this is not the World that God created centuries ago. There is some way, somehow it is different from the one with

Eden's Garden in it. The World now has hostility, selfishness, and resentments.

> The world no one is caring about; the other rather than themselves.
>
> The world where people laugh when you are in tragedy and are sad and angry when you have made it and are happy.
>
> The world where Humanity has become an expensive commodity to buy.
>
> The world where you wish to meet with an animal than a human being.
>
> The world where animals are more loyal companions than human beings.
>
> The world where you help and get returns to distroy you.
>
> The world where thank you and appreciation remains on the lips, while inside it is consumed with jealousy, envy and hostility.
>
> The world where God is like the neighbor next door; everyone should mind his/her business.
>
> The world where manipulation is the core virtue of business.
>
> The world where possession of destruction of humanity becomes the pride and symbol of power.
>
> The world where every forehead has the banner that says, "Trust me in your own risk."

The World where you don't know the difference of Church and a Social Hall.

The World where you don't even differentiate anymore between a male and a female. Gender has been liquefied. You can be whoever you want to be the next morning and trying to force people to acknowledge you as such.

The World where religion becomes just like one among many tribes.

This might not be the World the Great God created for His descendants. Perhaps somewhere, somehow, it was altered. Sometimes I am even not sure if I am walking on planet Earth where geography says human beings live or another planet. Perhaps Geologists have not noticed yet. We might have been moved to another planet.

The World where morals and ethical codes become old school for e-generation.

The World where wisdom is hidden in Ancient Books Archives and trust kept in museums.

The World where outward looks value you more than your inward potential.

The World where selfish is the Identity of every individual.

The World where the digital barriered the touch and humor of the human community.

The World where technology can create a shadow without the light.

> *The world where characters are being polished by money. In whatever the world would be, always be the man that brings sunshine to this world.*

Son, as your mother, I would tell you to be kind and gentle and that meekness is not really a weakness. But I came to realize that it is so hard to be gentle when you are victim. You need to experience and appreciate both hard and soft ways where in the hard way I could say you fight back, and you don't tolerate bullying depending on the situation. Hard way will expose you to adventures, danger, risks, and tell you it is ok to hit back, teach you to be a warrior and not a worrier and fighter and less coward. You are only a victim if you allow yourself to be one. Don't ever give a bully permission to torment you. On the flip side of the coin, soft way, be a defender, the one who will sit next to the loner in the back corner of the cafeteria and ignore the other popular kids' comments.

But you should also know people change as everything else changes. You have to have a stand on something. In this world, everything changes, every theory changes or is modified, people change, new theories and philosophies come and go, tried and believed. I am not telling you to not be resilient and accept change. I just tell you to have your own values and stand; that will guide you through it and you will not be waived or drifted away from your foundation.

11
CHURCH

In everything, put God first, and when you are successful, don't forget about God. In this COVID 19 era, church is not all about going to a specific building to worship. Currently, there are plenty of virtual worship services that you can just tune online wherever you are. It is good to plan something to make sure you are joined in the church community. If there are still buildings, and the situation is better, it is good to attend onsite worship services. Son, church is the place where you go to meditate about God with other people. You go to revitalize your faith with what is going on with your life.

I would love for you to know this, going to church is to rejuvenate your power, refuel yourselves and get a refill of your energy spiritually and mentally. Go to church in all-weather, son, in the rains and the sun, windy and snowing. Go to church whether it is a good day or bad day, whether you are happy or mad, poor or richer, young or old. Be involved in some programs of church when you can, get involved in the choir, in the boards, in the committee, have the role to play in the Kingdom of God. Preach the gospel with your actions, and just let words compliment the sermon that is already portrayed in your life.

12
PURPOSE-DRIVEN LIFE

Son, when you want to live a purpose-driven life, every single day matters. Every decision you make in a day matter. Be the best of you every single day for your joy, and enjoying seeing others have the best of you. You are given a day like a present. When you don't know what will happen, use every hour wisely. Every sunrise offers a second chance to have a beautiful page that your next chapter self will love to read.

Live a life of excellence. That doesn't mean a life without errors and withdrawals. Live the purpose-driven life. Have a goal for everything and always ask how you can make it and yourself better? That is how you will improve your life. This is the secret of growing and maturing. There are times you will reach your goals, celebrate and set another big goal. There are times you will need to sit and analyze what went wrong and how you can make it better. Have a goal of relationships. Examples: How many days are important in your relationships? Days like birthdays, anniversaries, etc., put them on your calendar. What day will you shut down everything just to be with people you love, what to do to spend quality time with the people you love. Have a goal of your health. How you are going to keep yourself fit? How many liters of water you will drink per day? How many sugars will you reduce per month? Have a goal of your education, whether you want to have a certificate or a Ph.D. and how to go about it. Have a goal of your fatherhood, how much time you will invest and teach your children. Have financial goals, business and how you are going to use your money and budgeting.

Have a goal of your husband hood, time to just listen to your wife, to just give your wife a treat, etc. Son, time is like a currency. It will give you profit and a good investment if you use it wisely. You are lost if you think there is someone who is cultivating your success, greatness, happiness, help, favor, and value. You are not entitled to any of that, although you can absolutely appreciate them when they are available. You are responsible for cultivating your best life. Son, I have never experienced seeing laziness benefit anyone, but I have seen that hard work pays people. The value of hard work is not only providing you with material things, but it gives you an opportunity to grow and be successful.

Son, invest in knowledge every single day. Try your

best to learn things every single day. The more you learn, the more you will have different perspectives of solving different puzzles of life. Read books, read documentaries, read journals, read, read, read. I don't know how many times I can emphasize to you about reading. But I just repeat again, read. If you can't read, listen to materials. Reading is good training for your imagination and thinking big. There is also more treasure in books, more keys to be discovered that will help you to unlock some doors in your life.

The best way to perform well in exams, tests and get good grades is by reading, studying, and listening. Reading pays a big role in learning and expanding your thinking ground. I always tell you, "Feed your brain with books and your soul with the bible," don't ever forget this because the tremendous impact is undeniable.

13
LEADERSHIP

Son leadership is the first to-do list God gave Adam, the task for Adam to do in this world. This doesn't matter if you are a mayor or a president. On the contrary, there are more politicians and men in power than leaders. Leadership is the skill that you will need in every phase of your life. Leadership skills are really not the same as management skills. The very rewarding position in this world is being the father, which means the leader of the family. There are things you cannot escape when you are a leader. Be a leader who raises your own pack and doesn't fall in line with what's predictable. Leaders serve; they are the first ones matching into the battle and the last ones to leave.

14
FINANCES

Sometimes money isn't everything, but it is something that you need in everything. Be an earner and a saver, a fan of frugality. Don't spend your money on useless things just to impress people that you shouldn't be trying to impress in the first place. Find value in work and acquiring knowledge, not trinkets, gadgets, women, or staff that will indeed end up owning you. Moreover, money helps you take care of your family and worry about other important things.

Become extremely good at something, develop, and shine a talent or gift you have. Practice everything, even greatness itself, because it's practice that yields results and not a talent. Practice makes it perfect. The value of mastering a skill is not necessarily what you earn from your skills but that you become great at it. The better you are at something, the more you are likely to get paid to do it.

Son, find money, get money, and save money, so that you can sleep better at night, and you don't have to worry about money, or paying bills. Son if you can, don't buy anything that you cannot pay cash for it.

The only thing you can not live without is oxygen, water, and food, but otherwise, you can live without all other things. You absolutely can live without a TV set, a fancy car, or a furniture set until you can pay for it.

Credits cards are a deception; I didn't say you shouldn't have them or use them, as you need them to build up your credit too. But all I am saying is, use them only when you have the money in the account to pay it back. In this country, the history of use and payments you have in these credits cards shows the world how responsible you are. It is also telling people your character and how much they can trust you. You must train your mind to know the difference between needs and wants. I don't need to tell you anything about spending, because spending is easy, it is saving that is hard. You must learn it as young as you should to develop the character.

Moreover, what goes with finances too is time. Be very prompt anywhere and everywhere you go. Arrive 30 to 15 minutes to the time of the appointment. It does not matter if it is a class, a date, a business appointment, an interview, work, or a meeting with a friend. It is the habit that will save you from a lot of misfortunes. Promptly will protect you from car accidents when you are trying to drive speedily because you were late, missing opportunities when you get there. At the same time, the deal is already done. You could good connections because you could not have time to meet and greet before the event. Other possibilities are missing your presentations because you did not have time to check them before time, losing your job because you have many tardinesses, or losing a job because you were late in an interview. Respect time because you cannot get it back or retrieve it, and it is most important to respect other people's time. There are accidents; make sure they don't become part and parcel of your character.

15
HEALTH

Son, I cannot finish these chronicles without talking about health. This is the most precious thing that you should protect and take care of, than anything else in this world. Health is wealth. It can make you save or make you spend a lot of money in your everyday life. Learn to take care of your body because you need it. Taking care of your body will not only help you be far away from unnecessary diseases but it also helps others not to have to take care of you at such premature age. The body has its way of communicating with you in its early stages when there is something wrong with it. Learn to hear its language. Respond to it before it's too late.

Son, eat well. It is good to start doing this as young as you can be because it will pay you back. Four diseases in the top ten causes of death in the United States are heart disease, cancer, stroke, and diabetes, which are the result of bad nutrition and unhealthy lifestyles. Health is life. You can have big dreams and end up in bed with them because of health complications. You should take it seriously because the fulfillment and accomplishment of your dreams depend on your health. There are a lot of people who died with their virgin dreams because they didn't pay attention with their health. Myles Munroe once said there is a wealth in the grave more than any other place because a lot of people have died with their dreams without having the time to accomplish them. If disregarding and doing things that will harm yourself is suicidal, then compromising about your health is the same as committing suicide. Son, health will rob your time to fulfill your dreams in this world. Just take good care of that God's temple.

SEE YOU LATER NOTE

Joshua Selman, a preacher from Nigeria, once said your name can be a key or padlock, your life will determine that. Yes, son, your name can be respected or trashed and ignored, your life will determine that. Let the world know you are here, and do it with passion, not to be famous but to be effective.

MY PRAYER

Father in heaven, I thank you for giving me such a precious reward. Thank you for the time that you entrusted me to bring forth such a great creation and raise him. Lord, I read, see, learn, and experience that you are a God of multitude grace and a great fixer. I pray that if there is anywhere I went wrong in raising him, anywhere that I was lazy in my role, please forgive me and fix that. I understand that it is my responsibility to discuss, teach, remind my children about your word as it says in Deuteronomy 6:6-8. I put my children unto your hands. Ooh Lord, be with them, help them, and guide them. As Hannah said, Lord for this child I have, I have lent him to the Lord. As long as He lives, he shall be lent to the Lord and worship the Lord. Lord, I pray for wisdom from you, to be the best mother I could be, to give them the knowledge, to show them the way, to help keep them safe and become all they were meant to be. In Jesus's name I pray.

Amen!

REFERENCES

1. Isaiah 49:15 (NKJV)
2. 1 Peter 2:9
3. Matthew 10:16 (NIV)
4. Psalms 8:4 (NKJV)

ABOUT THE AUTHOR

Edina Sichalwe Kuja is a mother of three boys and a wife of a brilliant man. A part-time writer and a gospel singer, she had a recorded Swahili gospel album known as Amenifuta Machozi, translated in English as 'God has wiped away my tears.'

In her other life, she has a Degree in Cultural Anthropology and Tourism from Tumaini University in Tanzania. She studied Planning and Project Management at the University of Dares Salaam in Tanzania. She has another Individualized Degree in Tourism, Mass Communication and Management at the University of Alabama. She works at the University of Alabama at Birmingham Hospital and is a nursing student at Herzing University in Alabama, United States.

www.ingramcontent.com/pod-product-compliance
Lightning Source LLC
Chambersburg PA
CBHW060428050426
42449CB00009B/2191